Thoughts and Feelings

Thoughts and Feelings

Success

Written by Susan Riley
Photos by David M. Budd

The Child's World®, Inc.

Published by The Child's World®, Inc.

Design and Production:
The Creative Spark, San Juan Capistrano, CA

Photos: © 1998 David M. Budd Photography

Library of Congress Cataloging-in-Publication Data

Riley, Susan, 1946–
    Success / by Susan Riley.
        p. cm. — (Thoughts and feelings)
    Summary: A child learns to tie shoes, climb a tree, zip a jacket, whistle,
in short, to be a success.
    ISBN 1-56766-676-0 (lib. reinforced : alk. paper)
    1. Success in children—Juvenile literature. [1. Success. 2. Child Development.]
I. Title. II. Series.
BF723.S77R55 1999
158.1—dc21
                                                            99-22621
                                                               CIP

If you ask who I am,

I will say, "I am me."

That's really much more
than just what you see.

I've learned quite a lot
by doing my best.

Why you might even say
I've become a success.

I no longer ride
my old purple trike.
Because now I can ride
a two-wheeler bike.

14

And I've learned to tie my
own shoes—just so!
Not simply in knots, but
in beautiful bows.

But it didn't come easy.
It didn't indeed.
I worked and I tried,
and I did succeed.

I can stand
on my head...

or climb up a tree.

And I've learned my alphabet

from A down to Z.

I can zip my own jacket...

24

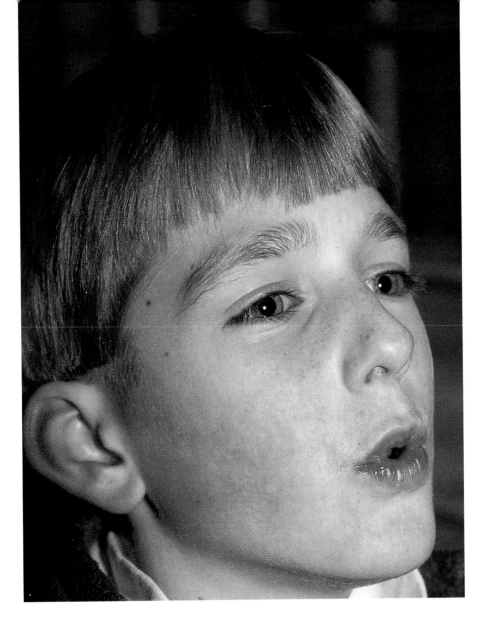

and whistle and hum.

Oh what a
SUCC

what a success
I've become.

And I'm proud of my success, of what I can do. You should be proud of what you can do, too.

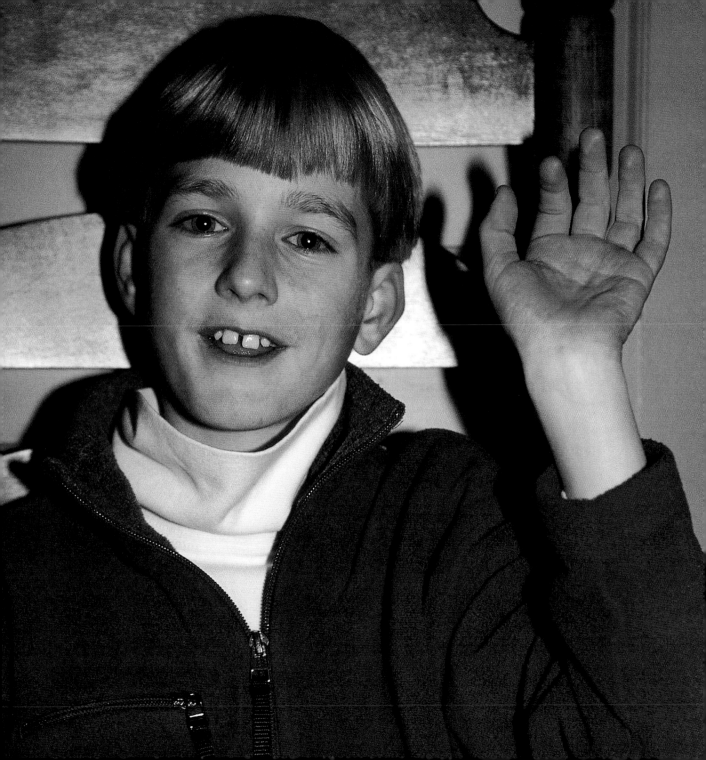

All of us have things that
we can do best,

and each of us has our own
kind of success.

For Further Information and Reading

Books

Penner, Fred. Proud. Marietta, GA: Longstreet Press, 1997.

Bernstein, Daryl. *Kids Can Succeed! 51 Tips for Real Life from One Kid to Another.* Holbrook, MA: Adams Media Corp., 1993.

Seuss, Dr. *Oh, The Places You'll Go!* New York: Random House, 1990.

Web Sites

For information about thoughts and feelings:
http://www.kidshealth.org/kid/feeling/

Read the story of a baby chick's success:
http://www.cts.com/crash/habtsmrt/barv/barv.htm

Fairy tales and stories about thoughts and feelings from all over the world: http://www.familyinternet.com/StoryGrowby/